Contents

To Alan, for endless patience.

Play Using Natural Materials

Welcome to *Play Using Natural Materials*, an exciting new publication which is part of the Ready, Steady, Play! series.

Get ready to enjoy a range of activities with your children, which will stimulate their all-round development.

The Ready, Steady, Play! books will help boost the confidence of new practitioners by providing informative and fun ideas to support planning and preparation. The series will also consolidate and extend learning for the more experienced practitioner. Attention is drawn to health and safety, and the role of the adult is addressed.

How to use this book

Play Using Natural Materials is divided into five main sections.

Section one (pp. 1–6) provides background information on using natural materials to support learning, looking at the history of their use and discussing the importance of first-hand experiences.

Section two (pp. 7–16) presents visual material to stimulate discussion with children in a group setting or one to one. Here you will find photographs of shells, pebbles and sea glass, together with examples of nature from gardens and hedgerows.

The activity section (pp. 17–68) encourages practitioners to help children explore natural materials through a range of different approaches, using all of their senses: handling, smelling, discussing and exploring a range of items or groups of items. All the activities have easy-to-follow guidelines.

The photocopiable pages in section four (pp. 69–81) help practitioners build on the learning aims of the set activities, or follow on from the discussion pages in the first section, and can be used in collecting evidence of developing skills and understanding, or to involve parents in what their child has been learning.

So read on, and enjoy ... Ready, Steady, Play!

Sandy Green
Series editor

Acknowledgements

To the children and parents of Cherry Class, St Philips CE Primary School, Bath.

To Madeleine (thanks for coming to play).

Series acknowledgement

The series editor would like to thank the children, parents and staff at:

- The Nursery, Wadebridge Community Primary School, Wadebridge, Cornwall
- Happy Days Day Nursery, Wadebridge, Cornwall
- Snapdragons Nursery, Weston, Bath, Somerset
- Snapdragons Nursery, Grosvenor, Bath, Somerset
- Tadpoles Nursery, Combe Down, Bath, Somerset

for allowing us to take photographs of their excellent provision, resources and displays.

Also to John and Jake Green, Jasmine and Eva for their help throughout the series, and to Paul Isbell at David Fulton Publishers for his patience, enthusiasm and support.

The Author

Alison Howe is an experienced early years teacher, currently Foundation Stage leader in a Primary school in Bath. She is also an Early Years Support Teacher working with Nursery and Pre-School practitioners for Bath and North East Somerset Local Education Authority.

Introduction

This title will focus on the great variety of play opportunities to be had through the use of natural and found materials. It will guide the reader through the potential of a range of different materials, promoting the inherent and distinctive value of each in turn. It will show the practitioner how she might support children's play and extend learning opportunities through a range of exciting experiences.

Why play and natural materials?

Practitioners who seek to provide quality play experiences for the children in their care might be forgiven for thinking that such activities can be best supported by purchasing from the ever-expanding range of equipment available from educational suppliers. In fact, within my own classroom I have a large variety of bright plastic objects designed to support children's learning; however, it would be wrong to assume that such manufactured aids are superior to seemingly more 'low-tech' alternatives. In this book I shall explore the play possibilities of resources to be found literally at our feet. The natural world is a bountiful source of inspiration that can provide exciting learning across the six areas of the Foundation Stage Curriculum.

Natural materials do not come with an instruction manual. Their uses and applications are only as limited as our imaginations. I hope this book will be a starting point for practitioners who will go on to explore the potential for themselves in their settings. Each piece of wood, each pebble, each fruit will have a unique shape, colour and texture to explore. It is this richness and variation that cannot be replicated by manufactured resources. I believe that providing children with natural materials will do more to foster curiosity than providing a toy or resource that evidently has a specific purpose usually predetermined by the adult mind. The toddler squeezing mud through his fingers in the garden or crunching through leaves in the park is exploring natural materials. As children grow older, that need for exploration does not diminish. It must be our job in the early years to foster and support this form of learning.

Through encouraging observation, exploration and questioning, the practitioner will also begin to develop in children important skills.

The tradition of play using natural materials

There is a long tradition of educating the early years with reference to the natural world. Scandinavian countries ensure that a majority of nursery education happens outside in the open. 'There is no such thing as bad weather, only bad clothing', goes the Norwegian saying.

Exploring the natural world is a vital starting point for much early education. Educator Eleanor Goldschmied (Goldschmied and Jackson 1994) promoted the idea of giving babies and young children purely natural materials with which to play, with her theories of 'heuristic play' and use of 'treasure baskets' for babies. This idea focused on the needs of babies and toddlers to make connections with the world around them. This, she argued, was best served by allowing them *real* objects to play with. She gave babies baskets filled with such delights as fir cones, balls of wool, lemons and wire whisks to form the 'treasure' of her 'treasure baskets'. Her research showed that children were far more engaged with play of this kind than with a selection of bright plastic items. If we are to build upon this fascination young children have with the natural rather than the manufactured then we must look at our own play provision.

Further support for using the real world for a play focus comes from the pre-schools of Reggio Emilia. This is an area in Northern Italy in which the community set up a collection of nurseries in the early 1960s. The education offered has since gained worldwide recognition, setting the standard for good early years practice. Art, design and creativity form the basis of the child-led curriculum. Art is supported by resident artists who foster the children's ideas and turn them into reality. One 'non-negotiable' is that the children have access to real materials at all times. Children are not given miniature, sanitised versions of the real world, but are immersed in the real world just as it is. 'Playdough' in vivid hues bears little resemblance to clay; plastic food is nothing like the real thing. Through natural playthings children come to learn about the world of which they are part, rather than forever be at a rehearsal of it.

Many of the activities in this book take place outside. The importance of exploring and fully using an outside environment, almost lost in the rush to 'educate' our young children, is at last being recognised. In an article 'Children's Outdoor Play and Learning Environments: Returning to Nature' White and Stoecklin (1998) extol the wonders of nature as explored by young children:

> All the manufactured equipment and all the indoor instructional materials produced by the best educator in the world cannot substitute for the primary experience of hands on engagement with nature.

Structure vs. freedom

The complexity and endless variety of the natural world leads to much more complex and open-ended play. Early experiences with the natural world lead to a development of imagination. They promote a sense of wonder and can act as a motivator to lifelong learning.

In the *Curriculum Guidance for the Foundation Stage* (QCA/DfEE 2000) it is suggested that children must develop:

> the crucial knowledge, skills and understanding that helps them to make sense of the world.

In order to do this, practitioners should pay attention to:

> activities based on first hand experiences that encourage exploration, observation, problem solving, prediction, critical thinking, decision making and discussion.

So, as educators of young children we would want to provide all the challenge, the wonder, the variety and open-ended discussion that working with natural materials can bring. But we must also make sure that our provision is based upon sound curricular principles.

The activities in this book range from the totally unstructured and free, to a rigid set of plans. We need to strike a balance in the play opportunities we provide. Within the most independent of child-chosen activities there lie teaching points that the skilled practitioner must identify and act upon.

Observing a child absorbed in play gives an adult many clues as to their learning. Sensitive intervention can lead a child on further. There are other activities which have much more clearly defined objectives, but these are still meant only as suggestions or starting points. A child used to being encouraged to question and be creative in his thinking will soon come up with his own set of suggestions beyond those thought up by any adult. There are no apologies for the frequent use of the word 'explore' in the activity outlines. Exploration, and with it the freedom to make mistakes, is key to learning in the early years.

Health, safety and environmental issues

Children must be allowed access to natural materials if they are to learn about and from them. Natural materials are not uniform. They cannot be guaranteed germ-free, smooth-edged and non-toxic. A few basic rules minimise risk. Always check materials for obvious hazards before giving them to the children. Always wash hands after handling the materials. Make a risk assessment of any outside area to be used (see photocopiable sheets on pp. 70 and 71). Use a reliable plant book to identify toxic plants and seeds.

Another consideration when using natural materials as playthings is the environment from which they come. Even at a very young age children need to begin to be aware that their actions have consequences upon their environment. This can start as simply as discussing the need for a litter-free area, but lead to more thought-provoking issues for them: 'What would happen if we picked all the flowers?'

The *Curriculum Guidance for the Foundation Stage* states as one of the early learning goals that children should 'Observe, find out about and identify features in the place they live and the natural world' and 'Find out about their environment, and talk about those features they like and dislike'. This is taken further by the initiative of 'Education for Sustainable Development' spearheaded by the QCA (www.qca.org.uk) which states:

> Sustainable development is the fundamental challenge that all societies face if we are to avoid long term damage to the Earth's basic life-support systems. Young people will be the decision-makers of the future, in both their personal and professional lives. They need to

learn to live in ways that increase quality of life for themselves and others without eroding the Earth's resources at a rate quicker than they can regenerate.

The activities in this book rely upon using the Earth's resources carefully. Children must be made aware of this and learn to treat the environment with respect if they are to begin to understand anything of sustainability. There are a few basic rules when engaging with nature: uproot nothing, keep to paths where possible and do not remove things from their place. This need not limit our enjoyment of these resources, however. Collecting a basket of conkers, fir cones or shells will not cause environmental damage. A cultivated area, which the children can use, provides an opportunity to teach the children something of sustainability. You have planted the garden so you can pick things, prune and dig. You can also replace them with new planting. Children who are involved with their outside environment in this way experience ownership and therefore take responsibility.

Use of ICT

The idea of working with natural materials seems initially to be at odds with promoting the use of technology to support this, but in fact technology can provide a further tool for learning in a number of ways. If we are faced with the question of how to preserve work done using natural materials the digital camera provides an answer. Natural materials are often not as durable as their manufactured counterparts. A child sorting leaves, weaving with flowers or building with pebbles cannot keep his work. A photograph provides the answer (and evidence for assessments). Digital cameras are ideal. Many are virtually 'childproof', allowing children to record their own efforts in this way. The photographs can be printed or displayed on a computer screen for all to share.

Use the Internet to allow children to explore the world beyond their immediate environment. If you are looking at a sunflower seed head then show them a field of sunflowers in France. Some excellent websites exist to support an environmental/natural theme (e.g. the 'Sebastian Swan' stories found on www.naturegrid.org).

Time-scales

As previously stated, these activities are intended to be flexible. Some of the activities could be completed quickly but many will take a full day or more. Much will depend upon the age, maturity and prior experience of the children. Once the children begin working in this way, learning to ask questions about what they see and what they discover, the activities will probably take longer. Allow children to dictate the time an activity takes (when practical to do so) and be ready to scaffold their learning, extending their questioning and teaching the skills they need. Developing an enquiring mind and being able to articulate their ideas are skills that will be called upon throughout their education and beyond.

The activities within this book will provide many purposeful play opportunities while covering a balanced early years curriculum, but most of all they will provide you and your children with a lot of fun. Watching a child experience 'awe and wonder' when faced with the natural world is something special.

References

Goldschmied, E. and Jackson, S. (1994) *People under Three: Young Children in Day Care*. London: Routledge.

Qualification and Curriculum Authority (QCA)/Department for Education and Employment (DfEE) (2000) *Curriculum Guidance for the Foundation Stage*. London: QCA.

White, R. and Stoecklin, V. (1998) 'Children's Outdoor Play and Learning Environments: Returning to Nature' (http://www.whitehutchinson.com/children/articles/outdoor.shtml).

Discussion resources

The following section provides a range of photographs to stimulate discussion with children, broadening their knowledge of natural materials.

Shells

Sea glass

Pebbles

Clay pieces

Leaves

Flowers

Dandelions

Seeds

Trees

Activities

The following pages contain twenty-five different activities suggesting a range of different ideas for play using natural materials. Each activity follows a standard format to ensure ease of planning and implementation:

- the resources needed
- the aim(s)/concept(s)
- the process
- group size
- health and safety
- discussion ideas/language
- extension ideas
- links to the Foundation Stage Curriculum.

Key to Foundation Stage Curriculum abbreviations:

SS   Stepping Stones

ELG   Early Learning Goals

PSE   Personal, social and emotional development

CLL   Communication, language and literacy

MD   Mathematical development

KUW Knowledge and understanding of the world

PD   Physical development

CD   Creative development

ACTIVITY 1

Clay interest table

Resources you will need

- A flat display surface
- A wide variety of clay objects, initially stored in a box out of view of the children. Try to include a mixture of forms both decorative and functional, fired and unfired, glazed and unglazed, differently glazed; fine porcelain, thick earthenware and so on. The children could add to the collection items they have made or brought from home

- Some unfired clay wrapped up to keep it moist and malleable
- Photographs of clay as seen in the environment (e.g. roof tiles, flowerpots)

Aims/concepts

- To begin to understand what materials objects are made from
- To sort and classify objects using independently chosen criteria
- To show an aesthetic appreciation for objects

Process

- Sit the children in a circle and explain that you have some things in your box that you would like to look at together.
- Remove objects from the box one by one. Allow the children to examine the objects, and encourage them to think about what the items are and what they might be made from: after some discussion explain that they all began as clay. Pass around a small ball of unfired clay for them to examine.
- Together, think of ways the objects might be sorted. You could sort by colour, shiny or matt, handle or no handle, fancy or plain and so on.
- Decide together how you will group the objects on the table.
- Allow the children to add to the display with objects brought from home.

Vocabulary/discussion

- Describe the objects: tall, short, round, square, heavier, lighter
- Discuss the similarities and differences in texture and pattern on your objects
- Encourage the children to say which of the objects they like best and why
- Encourage the children to talk through their reasons for sorting and classifying the objects in a particular way

Group size

Whole group

Extension idea

Re-sort the objects using different criteria.

Links to Foundation Stage Curriculum

SS Ask questions, often in the form of 'where' or 'what' (CLL)

ELG Interact with others, negotiating plans and activities and taking turns in conversation

SS Examine objects and living things to find out more about them (KUW)

SS Show an awareness of change

ELG Look closely at similarities, differences in patterns and change

SS Show curiosity and observation by talking about shapes – how they are the same or why some are different (MD)

ELG Use language such as 'circle' or 'bigger' to describe the shape and size of solid shapes and flat shapes

Health and safety

- ⚠ Children with skin conditions such as eczema may find handling the wet clay uncomfortable
- ⚠ Be aware of any chips or cracks in the objects causing sharp edges
- ⚠ Explain to the children that the objects are easily breakable and encourage them to take appropriate care when handling

ACTIVITY

2 Clay nature plaques

Resources you will need

- Clay (preferably air-drying clay)
- Outside area or a ready collection of leaves, twigs, petals, seed heads
- PVA glue

Aim/concept

- Children can make their own choice of natural materials to decorate their own clay plaque

Process

- Provide children with a small ball of clay, which they need to roll out into a flat oblong shape. Keep the clay fairly thick and help them to make it as even as possible.
- Either go out to an area where children can collect their own items for decoration, or let them choose from a ready collected source.
- The children can then press the leaves, seeds and so on gently and firmly into the clay, leaving an impression.
- The plaques should be left to dry out completely.
- When dry, the plaques can be varnished, or painted with PVA glue to provide a seal.
- While the clay is still soft, add a piece of bent wire to use as a hook for hanging the plaque.

Vocabulary/ discussion

- Talk about the changes in the clay as it dries out
- Encourage the children to pick a variety of decorating items
- Children can talk through their designs as they create them
- Ask them what they think may happen to soft, fresh leaves and flower heads as they are pressed into the drying clay

Group size

1:4

Extension ideas

1. Use some of the highly textured pieces of material and press firmly into the clay. Remove to leave behind an impression. This can now be filled with a small amount of plaster of Paris and left to dry before removing to create a raised image on a plaster plaque.
2. Completed plaques could be used as printing blocks.

Links to Foundation Stage Curriculum

KUW Ask questions about why things happen and how things work

CD Explore colour, texture, shape, form and space in 2- or 3D

PD Handle tools, objects and malleable materials safely and with increasing control

Health and safety

⚠ Ensure that items used for decorating plaques are non-toxic, non-irritant and not sharp

⚠ Clay work can irritate some skin conditions

ACTIVITY 3 Weaving with nature

Resources you will need

- Loom made from randomly stretched strings on a low display board (see photo), or ready-strung wooden or card frames
- A large variety of leaves, twigs, sticks, seed heads, petals, grasses and so on
- Bags or containers for collection of materials

Aim/concept

- For the class/group to work collaboratively to produce a weaving of materials found and collected in a local environment (school grounds, park, woodland). The weaving will become an expression of what the children have found out about this local environment

Process

- Show the children some weavings and the empty loom. Explain that the group is going to make a weaving in the classroom (10 minutes – whole group).
- Arrange time outside where the children can play and explore a suitable environment. Encourage the children to notice the variety of plant material around them. Following the health and safety guidelines (see below), allow the children to gather together materials (20–30 minutes – 1:6 ratio).
- Once back the classroom, unpack the collection and begin to weave the materials into the loom (10 minutes – 1:6 ratio). Some children may need considerable support to weave fragile material.
- Allow the children to add to the loom as they find new material over the following days.
- The weaving is likely to disintegrate after a week or two – but this could be a point for discussion. The materials need to be recycled – perhaps by returning them to where they came from or putting them on a compost heap.

Vocabulary/ discussion

- Leaf, stem, twig, flower, seed, weave, loom
- What can we find? Where did we find these things? What will happen to them?
- Describe colours, textures, feel and sound

Group size
1:6

Links to Foundation Stage Curriculum

KUW Investigate objects and materials, using all their senses as appropriate

CD Explore colour, texture, shape, form and space in 2- and 3D

PD Manipulate materials to achieve a planned effect

Extension idea
Children could make individual weavings on smaller looms.

Health and safety

⚠ Check that where you are going is a safe place for children to play. Check proximity to roads, climbing hazards and so on

⚠ Be aware of the environmental and safety issues associated with gathering plant material from public places (e.g. poisonous plants, thorns, protected species and hidden litter)

ACTIVITY 4 Mark-making on clay

Resources you will need

- Clay (either traditional or 'air-dry' clay)
- Rolling-pins
- Wipeable boards or protective cloth
- Aprons
- A variety of mark-making implements to include sticks, shells, cutlery, screws, nuts and bolts, washers, buttons, bottle tops, pebbles

Aim/concept

- Through structured play with the clay and tools provided, the children will begin to develop an understanding of the contrasting properties of the materials in their hands

Process

- Ensure that the clay is a suitable consistency for this work. It should be soft and malleable but not wet. A good guide is that a thumb can be easily pushed into the clay and come out clean.
- Give each child a piece of clay about the size of a tennis ball.
- Allow the children some time to play without adult direction.
- Introduce the collection of mark-making tools and demonstrate how a few might be used.
- Encourage the children to explore mark-making in a variety of ways and to share their discoveries with their peers.
- The time-scale of this activity may depend upon the children's previous experience with clay. It could be offered as an independent choice activity.
- Clay can either be reused after the activity (you may need to add a little water to the sack) or the results left to air-dry or fire. Once dry, the children could paint or varnish their work.

Vocabulary/discussion

- Push, pull, twist, pinch, press, mark, hard, soft, squidgy, crumbly
- Encourage the children to discuss the texture and feel of the materials. Note how the clay changes in texture as the activity progresses (as the children work the clay it will begin to dry and become harder and more crumbly)
- Discuss the marks and patterns made in the clay and how they were achieved

Group size

1:8

Links to Foundation Stage Curriculum

SS Explore malleable materials by patting, stroking, poking, squeezing, pinching and twisting them. Use simple tools to effect changes to the materials (PD)

ELG Handle tools, objects for construction and malleable materials with increasing control

SS Experiment to create different textures (CD)

ELG Explore colour, texture, shape and form in 2- or 3D

Extension idea

Children can begin to make regular or repeated patterns.

Health and safety

⚠ Children with skin conditions such as eczema may find working with clay uncomfortable and should wear disposable gloves

⚠ Care should be taken to supervise handling of sharp tools

⚠ Tools and surfaces need to be cleaned thoroughly to prevent a buildup of clay dust, which could be harmful

ACTIVITY 5 All sorts of seeds

Resources you will need

- A selection of seed heads (e.g. sunflower, poppy, nigella, clematis, conkers, acorns, sycamore and some seeds from fruits)
- Some seeds in packets, commercially produced

Aim/concept

- This activity introduces children to the cyclical nature of growth. The concept of seed dispersal is one that will be revisited in the National Curriculum science, and this opportunity for explorative play noting the different qualities of seeds provides a good foundation. Children are introduced to the idea of finding a good 'growing place', putting down roots, and growing and producing more seeds

Process

- Sit the children in a circle and look together at the variety of seeds you have collected.
- Do the children know what the seeds are? Where might they have come from? What are they for?
- Allow the children to discuss any experiences they have of seeds. Some may have encountered seeds in a packet, ready for growing. Show them the 'packet seeds' and explain where they have been collected from.
- Demonstrate the movement properties of the dandelion, clematis and sycamore.
- Go outside and let the children blow the seeds from dandelion and clematis heads, and to throw the sycamore seeds and watch them twirl as they fall.
- Display your collection of seeds and see if the children can add to them from seeds brought from home.

Vocabulary/ discussion

- Seed, root, shoot, plant
- Discuss how a seed is the beginning of a new plant
- Describe the movement of the seeds (e.g. float, spin, twirl)

Group size

Flexible

Extension ideas

1. Use a selection of non-fiction texts to show the growth cycle.
2. Look for evidence of seed heads or new growth outside.
3. Sort the seeds according to a variety of criteria.
4. Plant some quick-growing seeds, such as radish, in the garden.
5. Children can make paper spinners to emulate the movement of sycamore seeds (see photocopiable resource on p. 77).

Links to Foundation Stage Curriculum

KUW Investigate objects and materials by using all of their senses as appropriate. Ask questions about why things happen and how things work. Find out about, and identify, some features of living things, objects and events they observe

MD Show curiosity and observation by talking about shapes, why some are the same and why some are different

CLL Extend their vocabulary, exploring the sounds and meanings of new words. Show how information can be found in non-fiction texts to answer questions about where, who, why and how

Health and safety

⚠ Check that the outside area is safe for children to play
⚠ Be aware of the environmental issues associated with gathering plant material from public places (e.g. poisonous plants, thorns, protected species, hidden litter)
⚠ Wash hands after activity
⚠ Ensure that seeds are not eaten. Some seeds are edible (e.g. sunflower, pumpkin) but it is best to regard all seeds as inedible for this purpose

ACTIVITY 6 Hidden treasure

Resources you will need

- A variety of fruits and vegetables that have easily identifiable seeds inside. Try to include some that will be well known to the children, and some more unusual examples. A good collection might include apples, melon, kiwi, plum, squashes, avocado, peach and grapes
- A sharp knife
- Spoons
- Flat surface that can be easily cleaned
- Yoghurt pots or similar and compost (if extending activity)

Aims/concepts

- For children to *discover* that inside these fruits are seeds and to begin to understand that this is a means of growing more fruits
- To instil a sense of awe and wonder about the life cycle of plants

Process

- Allow the children to explore the selection of fruits while they are still intact. Encourage the children to smell, touch and shake them.
- Ask the children to guess what might be inside the fruits. Explain that no one will have ever seen inside these fruits before – that you are going to discover something new together.
- Begin with the fruits most familiar to the children in your group. Carefully cut open the fruit and pass around the cut halves. Were the predictions right?
- Continue to cut and expose the seeds and stones of the other fruits. Do they all look the same?
- Allow the children time to handle the seeds. Encourage conversation about the variety of textures and sizes of the seeds.
- Wash the seeds carefully (in a sieve) and allow the children to play independently, *or* extend the activity in one of the ways shown below.
- Cut up the fruit to share at snack time.

Vocabulary/discussion

- Fruit, vegetable, seed, pip, stone, plant
- Develop a sense of excitement and discovery as you cut open the fruits. Describe the fruits and the seeds together, encouraging words such as smooth, shiny, slippery, rough, bumpy, squashy
- If appropriate to the maturity of your group, you can begin to discuss how the seed is the starting point for a new plant/fruit to grow

Group size

1:8

Extension ideas

1. Once the seeds have been extracted and the children have had ample opportunity to explore them, you could plant the seeds in small yoghurt pots of watered compost.
2. Most sown seeds will produce some sort of shoot in a week or two, and some (such as citrus pips or avocado stones) can produce attractive indoor plants.
3. Washed and dried seeds can also be kept for counting, ordering, sorting and so on.

Links to Foundation Stage Curriculum

SS	Ask questions, often in the form of 'where' or 'what' (CLL)
ELG	Interact with others, negotiating plans and activities and taking turns in conversation
SS	Examine objects and living things to find out more about them (KUW)
ELG	Investigate objects and materials by using all their senses as appropriate
SS	Begin to talk about the shape of everyday objects (MD)
ELG	Use language such as 'greater', 'smaller', 'heavier' or 'lighter' to compare quantities

Health and safety

⚠ Care should be taken to supervise handling of sharp tools
⚠ Check beforehand for specific allergies to the fruits chosen (kiwi fruits in particular need checking)
⚠ Wash hands before and after the activity
⚠ Small seeds can be a choking hazard

ACTIVITY 7 Sensory walk 1. Look

Resources you will need

- Small unbreakable mirrors – one for each child
- Magnifying glasses – unbreakable
- It would be fun to use some binoculars if available
- Digital camera

Aim/concept

- Children (and more usually adults) will often walk a familiar route with little regard for the detail of things which are around them. Here the children are encouraged to explore in great depth, and in particular to look up and underneath to see what they discover! Although this activity may be done in any outdoor space it is often useful to use a familiar setting, as the children will then be encouraged to look in unfamiliar ways

Process

- Explain to the children that they are going on a special 'looking walk'. If you are using a familiar outside space ask the children what they think they might find there before you go out. These ideas can be scribed by an adult in a floor book to review together after the activity.
- Once outside, tell the children that they must spend some time looking up at the tops of trees and plants.
- Give each child a mirror and show them how to use it to look underneath hedges and bushes. What can they see reflected?
- If available, let each child look through some binoculars or through magnifying glasses.
- Turn stones to see what might be underneath.
- Allow the children to choose which images they would like to photograph.
- On returning to the setting reflect with the children on what they discovered. Do they compare to the jottings in the floor book? Were there any surprises? Print the photographs and allow the children to help display their favourites, or make up an album.
- Ask the children to describe their discoveries to other children, or to an adult who has not been on the 'looking walk'. Encourage them to include as much detail as possible in their accounts.

Vocabulary/discussion

- On returning indoors ask the children to describe what they discovered to other children or adults who have not been involved in the 'looking walk'. Encourage as much detail as possible in their explanations

Group size

1:6

Extension idea

Invite the children to make labels for their drawings and photographs.

Links to Foundation Stage Curriculum

KUW Investigate objects and materials using all their senses as appropriate. Find out about, and identify, some features of living things, objects and events they observe. Observe, find out about and identify features in the place they live and the natural world

CLL Use talk to organise, sequence and clarify thinking, ideas, feelings and events

CD Respond in a variety of ways to what they see, hear, smell, touch and feel

Health and safety

⚠ Check that the area to be used for the activity has been risk assessed

ACTIVITY 8

Sensory walk 2. Touch

Resources you will need

- Egg box for each child's collections
- Paper and wax crayons
- Collection of found materials

Aim/concept

- During this outside activity the children will have the opportunity to explore the environment using the sense of touch

---

Process

- Explain to the children that they are going on a special walk. This time, as well as using their eyes to see what is around them, they are going to use their hands to find out about what they discover. It may be a good idea to have had a previous activity exploring objects of differing textures so that the children have some clues as to the differences they might find.
- Once outside, allow the children some free time to explore. Hug a tree! Can they feel the rough bark against their faces as well as with their hands?
- Once the children have found something with a particularly interesting texture, show them how to make a rubbing using the paper and wax crayons.
- Ask the children to work with a partner and give each pair an egg box (with six spaces). Explain that they need to collect three pairs of objects (e.g. one hard one soft, one stiff one floppy, one smooth one rough).
- At the end of the activity, pool together the collections, and as a group sort and classify the objects found.

Vocabulary/ discussion

- Encourage the children to use appropriate words to describe textures (e.g. rough, smooth, lumpy, silky, soft, squishy)
- As a shared writing experience an adult can scribe a list of 'feely words'

Group size

1:6

Links to Foundation Stage Curriculum

KUW Investigate objects and materials using all their senses as appropriate. Find out about, and identify, some features of living things, objects and events they observe. Observe, find out about and identify features in the place they live and in the natural world

CLL Use talk to organise, sequence and clarify thinking, ideas, feelings and events

CD Respond in a variety of ways to what they see, hear, smell touch and feel

Extension ideas

1. Use a feely box in which an object from the explored environment has been placed. Can the children describe what they feel before guessing what the object may be? Can the children describe what they feel so that a friend might guess the object without feeling it himself?
2. Link the activity to a theme on 'senses'.

Health and safety

⚠ Check that area to be used for activity has been risk assessed

ACTIVITY 9

Sensory walk 3. Sound

Resources you will need

- Paper cones in a variety of sizes to use as ear trumpets
- A small tape-recorder
- Beaters
- Paper and pens

Aim/concept

- During this outside activity the children will have the opportunity to explore the environment using their sense of hearing

Process

- Ask the children to close their eyes. Once they are all sitting with their eyes closed make a loud and deliberate noise (e.g. banging a drum).
- Ask the children if they can tell you what you were doing. How do they know if their eyes were shut? Hopefully they will respond that they know because they heard you.
- Explain that you are going on a special 'listening walk'. As well as using their eyes to find out about what is around them the children will need to listen carefully for clues.
- Give the children beaters and show them how to tap trees, stones, run them through leaves and so on to compare the different sounds they make.
- Give the children the ear trumpets. Can they notice a magnification of sound?
- Stand silently for one minute and notice how many different sounds you hear. Traffic noise? Insects?
- Use the tape-recorder to record the sounds. Once back indoors, play the tape and see if the children can identify the sounds.

Vocabulary/discussion

- Encourage the children to use appropriate words to describe the sounds they hear (e.g roar, loud, quiet and rustle)
- An adult can scribe a list of 'sound words'

Group size

1:6

Extension idea

Make a 'sound map' of the area explored by sketching your route and drawing appropriate symbols for where certain noises were heard (e.g. leaves rustling, insects, cars).

Links to Foundation Stage Curriculum

KUW Investigate objects and materials using all their senses as appropriate. Find out about, and identify, some features of living things, objects and events they observe. Observe, find out about and identify features in the place they live and in the natural world

CLL Use talk to organise, sequence and clarify thinking, ideas, feelings and events

CD Respond in a variety of ways to what they see, hear, smell, touch and feel

Health and safety

⚠ Check that area to be used for activity has been risk assessed

ACTIVITY 10 Sensory walk 4. Smell

Resources you will need

- Small screw-top containers

Aim/concept

- During this outside activity the children will have the opportunity to explore the environment using their sense of smell

---

Process

- Prepare in advance a few containers (opaque film containers are ideal) of strong-smelling substances familiar to the children (e.g. peppermint essence, chocolate, lemon zest).
- Play a smelling game with the children. Can they guess what's in the container without looking? How?
- Explain that you are going on a walk and are going to be using your sense of smell to find out what's around you. Ensure that the area you are visiting has a good variety of 'smelly' plants. Herbs and flowering plants are best. Many public parks have a 'scented garden', which would be ideal as an initial experience.
- Encourage the children to smell all of the plants. Let them choose the smells they do and don't like. Encourage them to explain why.
- At the setting give the children some leaves, stems and flowers, which they can crush and then smell. Do they notice a stronger smell after crushing the plant?
- Let the children choose some of the plants to make perfumes or potions. Mix the plants with a small amount of water and crush down with a spoon. Keep a lid on the 'potion' and shake the mixture daily for about a week. Open the lid and smell again. Has it changed? Do the children like the smell?

Vocabulary/discussion

- Encourage the children to use appropriate words to describe the smells
- Make a list of smells the children do and don't like

Group size
1:6

Extension idea
Link with a larger theme on senses.

Links to Foundation Stage Curriculum

KUW Investigate objects and materials, using all their senses as appropriate. Find out about, and identify, some features of living things, objects and events they observe. Observe, find out about and identify features in the place they live and in the natural world

CLL Use talk to organise, sequence and clarify thinking, ideas, feelings and events

CD Respond in a variety of ways to what they see, hear, smell, touch and feel

Health and safety

⚠ Check that area to be used for activity has been risk assessed
⚠ Check children for allergies to pollen and so on before allowing them to smell the plants
⚠ The 'potions' or 'perfumes' are best not applied to the skin in case of reaction

Resources you will need

- Small paper bag for each child

Aim/concept

- This is a simple activity, which provides a focus for playing outside. Children are encouraged to look closely at what lies around them. This activity also encourages counting skills

Process

- Give each child a paper bag.
- Ask the children to collect a given number of different objects in their paper bag. Give examples to the children of suitable objects (e.g. different leaves, fir cones, pebbles, twigs).
- Back inside, compare the children's collections. Can they count out each object and count them back into their bags?
- What can they tell you about each object?

Vocabulary/ discussion

- The same/different, how many? More/less
- Encourage the children to describe the things they have found. Which is their favourite? Why?

Group size

1:6

Extension ideas

1. The number of objects to be found by the children can vary to differentiate the activity. Children can match the numbers of objects found to numerals.

2. Ask the children to choose one of their objects and to hide this outside again. Could they describe it for a friend to find, or find it themselves another day?

3. Ask the children to each find a stick. Back inside, the children need to study their own stick and really get to 'know' it. After this the sticks are all bundled together. Can the children identify their own stick among the bundle?

Links to Foundation Stage Curriculum

KUW Investigate objects and materials, using all their senses as appropriate

MD Say and use number names in order in familiar contexts. Count reliably up to ten everyday objects

Health and safety

⚠ Check that the designated collection area has been risk assessed and that the children are clear about guidelines for the activity

⚠ Wash hands after the activity

ACTIVITY
12 Nature palettes

Resources you will need

- Small pieces of white card, one for each child. These may be cut out in the shape of mini-artists' palettes to add a bit of fun
- Double-sided sticky tape
- An outside area with a variety of planting

Aim/concept

- This activity encourages children to look closely at the environment around them and to realise the variety that can be found. It can be differentiated to suit the age or experience of the children (e.g. restrict the number of samples found, limit the colour palette)

Process

- Prepare each piece of card by placing two or three strips of double-sided sticky tape on one side only.
- Show the prepared cards to the children and explain that they are going to hunt for tiny scraps of plant material to stick on their card.
- Decide on the collection criteria for the children. They could either look for a variety of different colours to add to their palette, restrict collection to many shades of green or perhaps go on a 'rainbow' walk hoping to find a sample for each colour of the rainbow. Make sure the collection area has been checked first to ensure that this will be possible.
- This activity requires a considerable level of manual dexterity, so young children may need assistance in placing their samples on the card.
- Encourage the children to use either found materials or small scraps of plants (e.g. a piece of a leaf, one or two daisy petals). Explain that nothing is to be uprooted.
- Come together as a group and compare the palettes. How much variety can be seen?

Vocabulary/discussion

- Take time to look at and discuss subtle differences in shades (e.g. 'these are all green but they are all different')
- Encourage discussion about the variety of colours found

Group size

1:6

Links to Foundation Stage Curriculum

KUW Investigate objects and materials, using all their senses as appropriate. Look closely at similarities, differences and change

MD Work creatively on a small scale. Explore colour, texture, shape, form and space in 2- or 3D

Extension idea

Older children can try to match the colours found for their palettes by mixing paints.

Health and safety

⚠ Check designated collection area to ensure that there are no irritant, poisonous or prickly plants
⚠ Wash hands after the activity

13 Natural sculptures

Resources you will need

- A collection of similarly shaped leaves, petals, sticks, stones, seeds and so on
- A camera to record your work

Aim/concept

- Children use natural, gathered materials to create patterns laid out on the ground. As these sculptures are ephemeral in nature it is a good idea to photograph the completed sculptures to avoid disappointment the next day when they may well have disappeared!

Process

- A good starting point before attempting to make your own natural sculpture is to look at the work of artist Andy Goldsworthy. Explain to the children that the bold, vivid patterns and shapes he creates are made from leaves, petals, stones and so on that he has gathered together. Explain that he uses no scissors or glue. Ask the children what they think will happen to the 'sculptures' over time. Explain that he photographs all of his work as it cannot be kept or moved, and that you will do the same.
- Take the children outside. You will need to be able to amass a considerable amount of similar natural material for your sculptures, so check your chosen area beforehand. Woodlands are ideal, since material can usually be gathered easily without resorting to picking growing plants.
- Adults should work together with the children, helping them to place their chosen material close together for the best effect. Keep stepping back from your work so that you can view it properly.
- Don't forget to take photographs of the finished sculptures. It is nice to remind the children that all the materials used for your sculpture will go back to being part of the natural environment. You have taken nothing away – just moved its position for a while.

Vocabulary/discussion

- Use mathematical language to describe shape (e.g. curved, straight, circle) and positional language (e.g. next to, behind, on top)
- Encourage the children to describe the textures of the materials they are using, the colours, light and shade, glossy or matt
- Ask the children to think of a title for their work

Group size

1:4

Extension idea

Children can work individually to make sculptures.

Links to Foundation Stage Curriculum

CLL Interact with others, negotiating plans and activities. Use talk to organise, sequence and clarify thinking, ideas, feelings and events

KUW Investigate objects and materials, using all their senses as appropriate. Look closely at similarities, differences, patterns and change. Build and construct with a wide range of objects, selecting appropriate resources, and adapting their work as necessary

CD Explore colour, shape, form and space in 2- and 3D

MD Talk about, recognise and re-create simple patterns. Use everyday words to describe position. Use language such as 'circle' or 'bigger' to describe the shape or size of solid shapes or flat shapes

Health and safety

- ⚠ Check that all plant materials are non-toxic and free of thorns
- ⚠ Do a risk assessment of your chosen area
- ⚠ Ensure that the children wash their hands after the activity

14 Seed tray gardens

Resources you will need

- A clean seed tray (or similar-sized container)
- Compost
- A large collection of plant materials, gravel, small wooden sticks, small figures, pebbles and small stones
- Add a small piece of mirror or foil to create 'water' (optional)

Aims/concepts

- Children enjoy the idea of making a miniature version of something they know well, using small pieces of plant materials and stone to make a garden of their own
- Although this activity requires a great deal of adult support, even very young children can be left to 'plant' according to their own design wishes

Process

- Show the children a selection of garden photographs from books or magazines. Point out major features of the gardens.
- Look at any garden attached to your setting and explain that the space was planned. Again notice different features.
- Show the children an empty seed tray. Explain that you are going to make a tiny garden in the tray. Add compost in a thin layer, then perhaps a gravel 'path'. Let the children pick out pieces for you to 'plant' as trees and shrubs.
- Once the children have seen an adult modelling making a 'garden', they can make their own. Adults may well be needed to help keep some 'planting' stable.
- Children may like to add figures or animals from small world-play equipment to their garden.
- You could have a 'gardens exhibition', and invite parents and other visitors to view the children's gardens.
- If sprayed with water regularly, the gardens should keep fresh for about a week.

Vocabulary/ discussion

- Talk about pattern and form
- Encourage the children to explain their choices for their design
- Encourage the use of mathematical language to describe shape (e.g. straight, curved) and position

Group size

1:4

Extension idea

Older children may like to design a garden with a particular theme (e.g. a garden for wildlife, a garden for children, a colour theme).

Links to Foundation Stage Curriculum

KUW Investigate objects and materials, using all their senses as appropriate

CD Explore colour, shape, form and space in 2- and 3D

MD Talk about, recognise and re-create simple patterns. Use everyday words to describe position. Use language such as 'circle' or 'bigger' to describe the shape or size of solid shapes or flat shapes

Health and safety

⚠ Check that all plant materials are non-toxic and free of thorns
⚠ Use sterile, bagged compost

ACTIVITY 15 Working with withies

Resources you will need

- Withies are long, flexible willow twigs. They are fairly cheap to buy, so provide a large bundle for the children to use, along with masking tape, string or flexible wire to join them. A pair of pliers is also useful. Withies have a long 'shelf life' but they can begin to dry out if kept for a long time. Soak overnight to maximise their flexibility

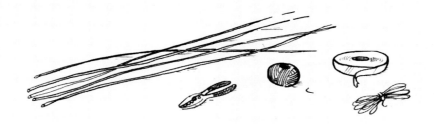

Aim/concept

- Children are very used to working with a variety of commercially available construction kits. Although these have a place, the fact that the component parts are fixed in shape and size can limit creativity in their use. Using withies as a construction resource can allow the children the freedom to create a variety of shapes, and to work on a large scale

Process

- Allow the children free time to play with the withies, to explore their properties.
- Once the children have had ample opportunity to play with the withies, introduce the idea of joining them together (a simple teepee shape is perhaps the easiest starting point). The initial joining can be done most simply using masking tape, but this may need to be reinforced with string or garden wire.
- Encourage children to work collaboratively – one holds the structure in place while another joins it with tape.
- An adult should have access to a pair of pliers to encourage tighter bends if required.
- Finished structures can be left just as they are, or decorated with tissue paper, fabric, feathers and so on.

Vocabulary/discussion

- Use mathematical language to describe shape (e.g. curved, straight, and the names of solid shapes)
- Describe the withies: 'bendy, flexible'
- Do children working collaboratively with the withies take turns and negotiate in their conversations?

Group size

Flexible

Links to Foundation Stage Curriculum

CLL Interact with others, negotiating plans and activities

KUW Build and construct with a wide range of objects, selecting appropriate resources, and adapting their work as necessary. Select the tools and techniques they need to shape, assemble and join materials they are using

CD Explore colour, shape, form and space in 2- and 3D

MD Use language such as 'circle' or 'bigger' to describe the shape or size of solid shapes or flat shapes

Extension ideas

1. Children can use their structures as a basis for weaving.
2. Children can make structures big enough to go inside.

Health and safety

 Withies are non-toxic and fairly soft. Remind the children, however, to be aware of the length of them when working

ACTIVITY 16 Natural or not?

Resources you will need

- A collection of objects for the children to sort, including fruit and vegetables, seeds, pebbles, plants, fir cones and manufactured objects (e.g. a plastic brick, sorting shapes, beads)

Aims/concepts

- Being able to classify is an important scientific skill; this is a good early introduction
- Limit the objects to easily identifiable natural or non-natural items and leave out anything ambiguous (e.g. paper)

Process

- Sit the children in a circle and place the objects for sorting in the middle.
- Tell the children that the objects need to be sorted out and begin by explaining your criteria: that you want to put all of the items which you might find while on a walk in one pile, and all of the things that someone had to make in another.
- Allow the children to sort the objects, giving their reasons for their decisions.
- Let the children look around the room and the garden to find objects of their own to add to the collections. Make sure that they have access to items indoors which came originally from outside (e.g. a collection of shells or some sand).

Vocabulary/discussion

- Depending upon the prior experiences of the children, the correct scientific vocabulary can be introduced (e.g. 'natural' and 'manufactured')
- Encourage the children to give reasons for their sorting

Links to Foundation Stage Curriculum

KUW Investigate objects and materials by using all of their senses as appropriate. Ask questions about why things happen and how things work. Find out about, and identify, some features of living things, objects and events they observe. Talk about, recognise and re-create simple patterns. The kinds of objects that the children sort can be made more difficult to classify according to their prior experiences. A wooden object initially bears little relation to a tree growing in the garden. Introduce a silk flower alongside a real one and see if the children can differentiate. This kind of activity leads into skills needed for the KS1 science curriculum

Group size

Flexible

Health and safety

⚠ Wash hands after activity

ACTIVITY 17 Going on a bear hunt

Resources you will need

- Copy of *We're Going on a Bear Hunt* by Michael Rosen and Helen Oxenbury
- Plastic container of 'mud' – sterile compost mixed with water with a bit of clay added makes good 'mud'
- Plastic container of grass clippings, long spiky leaves, spikes of corn and so on
- Bowl of water
- Large plant (or, even better, several)
- Container of ice-cubes
- Dark fabric used to drape over tables to use as a 'dark cave'
- A teddy bear

Aim/concept

- This activity requires quite a lot of forward planning and setting up by an adult. It does, however, give an added dimension to a favourite story. Children who are familiar with the story *We're Going on a Bear Hunt* will enjoy sharing the experiences of the protagonists in this way. No amount of dramatising the story using imaginary mud, grass and ice is anywhere near as much fun as exploring the real thing

Process

- Read through the story several times so that the children are familiar with the sequence of events.
- Explain that you are going on a bear hunt of your own. Reassure the children that they will be quite safe because you will meet a friendly bear. Some children can become anxious at the thought of an encounter with a bear!
- Lead the children around the various substances. Follow the sequence of the story. If space allows, the containers could be large enough for the children to step in as if walking through the water or mud, peeking round the large plants (the big dark forest), but if not they can explore the materials with their hands.
- Allow the children their own time to explore each container, or to go back to a favourite. The containers could be left out all day for the children to explore.
- When you reach the 'cave', build up the excitement of what you might find. Be prepared for lots of shrieks, even when they discover a friendly teddy is their bear!

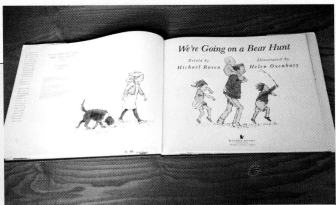

Vocabulary/discussion

- Repeat the refrain from the story: 'We're going on a bear hunt, we're going to catch a big one...' Children enjoy the pattern and rhythm
- Encourage descriptive language as children explore the story
- Refer back to the description contained in the story

Group size

1:6

Extension idea

Children can make zigzag books with a page to represent each element of the story (e.g. a 'muddy' picture, a 'grassy' picture).

Links to Foundation Stage Curriculum

CLL Listen with enjoyment, and respond to stories, songs and other music, rhymes and poems, and make up their own stories, songs, rhymes and poems. Extend their vocabulary, exploring the meaning and sounds of new words. Use language to imagine and re-create roles and experiences. Retell narratives in the correct sequence, drawing on language patterns of stories

KUW Investigate objects and materials by using all of their senses as appropriate

PD Move with confidence, imagination and safety

CD Use their imagination in art and design, music, dance, imaginative and role-play, and stories

Health and safety

⚠ Do not use mud from the garden, as it cannot be guaranteed to be free of harmful substances
⚠ Check that plants used are non-toxic
⚠ Wash hands after the activity

ACTIVITY 18 Woodland folk

Resources you will need

- Large collection of petals, leaves, grasses, twigs, feathers, flat pieces of bark
- PVA glue and brushes or spreaders
- Drawn figure for dressing (see photocopiable sheets on pp. 72 and 73)

Aim/concept

- This fun activity involves using gathered materials from the garden for dressing figures as fairies or pixies

Process

- Discuss the children's ideas of fairies and pixies. Where might they live? What do they do all day? Discuss what they might wear. For inspiration you might like to look at books containing illustrations of fairyland people (e.g. *Fairie-ality* by Eugene Bird *et al.* gives stunning examples of fairies and pixies dressed in natural materials).
- Give each child a figure template. It's nice to have a selection of pixies, elves and fairies.
- With the children, sort through the materials you have with which to dress the figures.
- Encourage the children to lay out their selections before gluing into place.
- Some of the petals may be quite fragile, so explain to the children that they need to take great care in handling them.
- Adult assistance may be needed to handle and glue the more delicate items.

Vocabulary/discussion

- Children can really use their imaginations when talking about fairies. Encourage them to be inventive. What are they dressing their fairy for? Is it a special event?
- When using the material for dressing the fairy ensure that the children know the names of items they are using (e.g. bark, petal, stem). Introduce the words 'delicate' and 'fragile'. You could also introduce the idea of camouflage

Group size

1:6

Extension ideas

1. The children could be involved with the collection of materials which are used for dressing their figures.
2. The finished figures can be used as a basis for story-telling and role-play.
3. The finished figures can be taken outside and placed in their 'natural surroundings'.

Links to Foundation Stage Curriculum

CLL Extend their vocabulary, exploring the meanings and sounds of new words. Use language to imagine and re-create roles and experiences

KUW Select the tools and techniques they need to shape, assemble and join the materials they are using

PD Handle tools, objects, construction and malleable materials safely and with increasing control

CD Explore colour, texture, shape, form or space in 2- or 3D. Use their imagination in art and design, music, dance, imaginative and role-play, and stories. Express and communicate their ideas, thoughts and feelings by using a widening range of materials, suitable tools, imaginative and role-play, movement, designing and making

Health and safety

⚠ Ensure that all material used is non-toxic and thorn-free

ACTIVITY
19 Mix it up

Resources you will need

- Large containers of seeds, dried peas, beans, lentils, rice, loose tea, porridge oats and so on
- Scoops, spoons and measures
- Plates and mixing bowls

Aim/concept

- This activity allows children to explore the textures and consistencies of a variety of dried ingredients for play cooking. Although they won't produce anything edible, they will love the freedom of making their own mixtures, and the process. It gives a touch of realism to role-play cooking as they are using real food items

Process

- Arrange containers of your chosen 'ingredients' in the centre of a table or other easily cleaned area.
- Give each child a mixing bowl.
- Allow them freedom to add their own choice of ingredients to their bowls and mix away.

Vocabulary/discussion

- Children engaged in this activity are continually exploring the properties of the materials. Encourage them by appropriate questioning: 'What will this do to your mixture?', 'What should we add now?'
- This is a good opportunity to encourage mathematical development. Count the numbers of scoops added. Talk about quantities (e.g. 'What did you add most/least of?')

Group size

1:4

Extension ideas

1. Children could try to record their 'recipes' and tell another child how to make something.
2. Children could make something with a particular purpose in mind (e.g. dinner for dolly).

Links to Foundation Stage Curriculum

CLL Interact with others, negotiating plans and activities and taking turns in conversation. Use talk to organise, sequence and clarify thinking, ideas, feelings and events

KUW Investigate objects and materials by using all their senses as appropriate. Build and construct with a wide range of objects, selecting appropriate resources, and adapting their work as necessary. Ask questions about why things happen and how things work

CD Respond in a variety of ways to what they see, hear, smell, touch and feel. Express and communicate their ideas, thoughts and feelings by using a widening range of materials, suitable tools, imaginative and role-play, movement, designing and making

MD Use developing mathematical ideas and methods to solve practical problems. In practical activities and discussion, begin to use the vocabulary involved in adding and subtracting

Health and safety

⚠ Ensure that the children do not attempt to eat their mixtures. Uncooked beans can contain toxins

⚠ Wash hands after the activity

ACTIVITY
20 Compost tray

Resources you will need

- Small plastic trays (seed trays or slightly larger; a full-sized sand tray is usually too large)
- Bags of clean sterile compost (N.B: Do not use 'homemade' compost)
- Watering cans, 'sand toys'

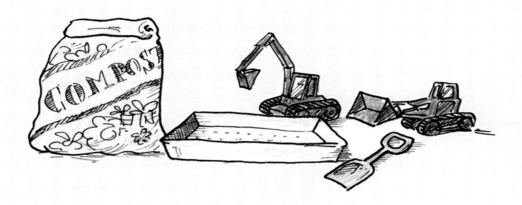

Aim/concept

- Children are usually quite familiar with playing with sand. Substituting sand with compost provides a totally different sensory experience. It provides a clean and safe way to replicate playing with garden soil, which may be contaminated, using sterile compost

Process

- Provide a tray filled with compost, watering cans, 'sand toys', toy tractors and so on.
- Allow the children free exploration time.
- Encourage the children to explore both dry and wet compost. Let the children add water gradually and note how it changes. How much water will they need to add in order to make mud?
- Leave wet compost in a warm place to see how long it takes to dry out.
- Discuss with the children the differences between compost and sand.

Vocabulary/discussion

- Dry, crumbly, sloppy, squish, sloppy, powdery
- Encourage the children to describe what they feel

Group size

Maximum 3 per tray

Extension idea

Add other 'garden' products to the compost to change the texture, such as gravel or small pebbles.

Links to Foundation Stage Curriculum

KUW Investigate objects and materials using all their senses as appropriate. Look closely at similarities, differences and changes. Ask questions about why things happen

MD Use language such as 'greater', 'smaller', 'heavier' or 'lighter' to compare quantities

CLL Use talk to organise, sequence and clarify thinking, ideas, feelings and events

Health and safety

⚠ Use only clean 'garden centre' compost

ACTIVITY 21
Laminated leaves and leaf match

Resources you will need

- Large selection of leaves
- Laminating machine
- Pouches

Aim/concept

- The huge varieties of leaf colour and shape provide an excellent resource for use in many ways across the curriculum. There is always a place for children to handle and play with leaves in their natural state, though their life as a play material is short. However, this provides a long-lasting resource. The leaf-match activity may be used as part of a wider theme looking at Autumn leaves and colour; the activity is just as valid using fresh leaves

Process

- Collect a selection of leaves in a variety of sizes, shapes and colours.
- Laminate the leaves leaving space between each one.
- Cut out each leaf round the laminated shape.
- Use the resource for children to count, sort, pattern, make and classify. Change the criteria according to the experience of the children (e.g. by colour, shape, whether jagged or smooth-edged).
- Choose a selection of leaves and laminate A4 'mats' of these selections.
- Show the 'mat' to the children. Discuss the shapes, shade, variety of the leaves.
- Go outside (to your previous leaf-collection area) and give each child a 'mat' of their own.
- The children can now go and find leaves to match the ones on their individual 'mat'.

Vocabulary/discussion

- Leaf, stem, colour, shade, lighter, darker, smooth, jagged
- Describe colours, shapes
- Pattern, sort, what comes next? Bigger, smaller, how many? What can we find? Where did we find these things?
- Describe colours, shapes: exactly/almost the same

Group size

Flexible

Extension ideas

1. Allow the children free play with the leaf collection and observe how they choose to use them. A strategically placed adult can make notes on the children's activities without controlling their play.
2. Children could be involved in the original collection of material, making a 'mat' for a friend to use for matching.

Links to Foundation Stage Curriculum

KUW Investigate objects and materials using all their senses as appropriate

CD Explore colour, shape, form and space in 2- and 3D

MD Show curiosity and observation by talking about shapes, how they are the same or why some are different

Health and safety

⚠ Check that the laminating machine is kept away from children
⚠ The laminating of leaves and cutting out should be carried out by an adult
⚠ Check that outside area has been risk assessed

ACTIVITY

22 The three little pigs

Resources you will need

- Clay, both in its natural state and fired (ideally pieces of broken tile)
- Straw
- Twigs or small sticks
- Pieces of card
- PVA glue

Aim/concept

- This traditional tale may be used as a starting point to explore the properties of the building materials chosen by the pigs. With support, the children could begin to evaluate the suitability of the materials for building

---

Process

- Read or tell the story of *The Three Little Pigs* up until when the pigs have built their houses but *before* the wolf comes! Can the children remember the different materials that the pigs chose to build their houses from?
- Show the children the examples of the building materials. Look at the clay in its natural state and as fired tiles.
- Encourage the children to explore the materials. Which would be best? Why?
- Read to the end of the story using the 'building' materials as props.
- Let the children glue the straw, sticks and tile pieces on to pieces of stiff card.
- When dry, examine the card pieces and see which appears most suited for the purpose.
- The card pieces may be used as part of a display.

Vocabulary/discussion

- Strong, weatherproof, weak, fragile
- Encourage the children to give reasons for their choices of best building materials. Why was the wolf able to blow down the straw house easily?
- If the children were to build a house, what materials would they use?

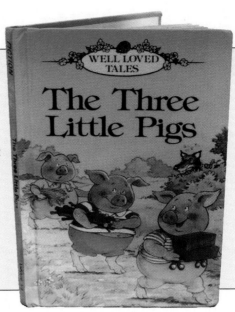

Group size

1:15

Extension ideas

1. Children could make their own recycled models of the pigs' houses using the straw, twigs and tiles to decorate the outside.
2. Link to a topic on homes or buildings.

Links to Foundation Stage Curriculum

`KUW` Observe, find out about and identify features in the place they live and in the natural world. Investigate objects and materials, using all of their senses as appropriate

`CLL` Sustain attentive listening, responding to what they have heard with relevant comments, questions or actions. Listen with enjoyment, and respond to stories

`PD` Handle tools, objects, construction and malleable materials safely and with increasing control

Health and safety

⚠ Check that the sticks/twigs and tile pieces have no obvious sharp edges
⚠ Ensure children with skin complaints such as eczema are comfortable handling clay

ACTIVITY 23 Some ideas for sand play

Resources you will need

- Sand in a container
- Water, small world toys, shells, dried pulses, rice, pebbles, powder paint, glue, sticks, stones, scrapers, combs

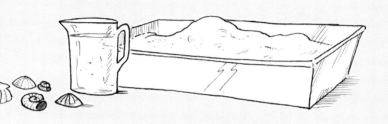

Aim/concept

- As with the water tray, sand is an integral part of any early years setting. Children are happy to play with a bowl of sand, often with nothing added at all, simply exploring and enjoying the properties of the material. It is important to sometimes leave the sand just as it is, but fun to add new experiences from time to time

Process

- Vary the sand from bone-dry and free-flowing to just damp and able to mould, to completely waterlogged and a fun, sloppy mess.
- Add a variety of small world toys (cars, animals, people) so that the sand may be sculpted into roadways, villages, dens and so on.
- Use combs, sticks and so on to make patterns in the sand. This works well, and gives different results in both damp and dry sand.
- Add a variety of containers that can serve as moulds.
- Add powder paint to the sand to change the colour.
- Bury 'treasure' in the sand (e.g. old pieces of jewellery, shiny plastic beads) and tell the children to dig for it!
- Add wooden blocks, fir cones, cotton reels and other objects, which the children can use to make impressions in damp sand.
- Draw a pattern on paper, go over the outline with glue and use dry sand to sprinkle on to make a sand picture.
- Add a quantity of uncooked rice, dried pulses, gravel or pebbles to the sand to add texture.
- Add shells to the sand to give a 'seaside' experience.

Vocabulary/discussion

- Independent play with sand gives practitioners an ideal opportunity to observe the children. Can they take turns and negotiate? Do they problem-solve?
- Sensitive adult intervention can focus the children upon exploring the properties of the material, to develop mathematical language of measure, use talk to imagine small world scenarios and so on

Group size

Flexible

Extension ideas

1. Link to a topic on sand in homes (e.g. sand turtles, camels, crabs). These could be researched using the Internet.
2. Explore the textures of sandpaper with the children. How do the different 'grades' differ in appearance, texture and so on?

Links to Foundation Stage Curriculum

CLL Interact with others, negotiating plans and activities and taking turns in conversation. Extend their vocabulary, exploring the sounds and meanings of new words. Use language to imagine and re-create roles and experiences. Use talk to organise, sequence and clarify thinking, ideas, feelings and events

KUW Investigate objects and materials by using all their senses as appropriate. Build and construct using a wide range of objects, selecting appropriate resources and adapting their work as necessary. Ask questions about why things happen and how things work

CD Respond in a variety of ways to what they see, hear, smell, touch and feel. Express and communicate their ideas, thoughts and feelings by using a widening range of materials, suitable tools, imaginative and role-play, movement, designing and making

MD Use language such as 'circle' or 'bigger' to describe the shape or size of solid shapes or flat shapes. Use everyday words to describe position

Health and safety

⚠ Children need to be aware of basic safety rules when playing with sand (e.g. no flicking or throwing sand, do not put it into mouths)

⚠ Be aware of children with skin conditions such as eczema

ACTIVITY
24 Ideas for water play

Resources you will need

- Glitter, food colouring, clay, soap flakes, balloons, rubber gloves, ice-cube trays, cornflour (resources are only as limited as your imagination!)

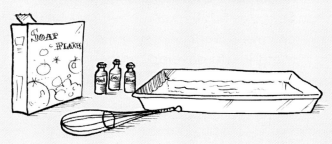

Aim/concept

- The water tray is a standard piece of furniture in every early years setting. It is often filled with plastic toys that provide great learning opportunities. Often, however, the most fun can be derived by adding much more 'low-tech' additions, or by altering the state of the water itself

Process

- Add a couple of handfuls of glitter to the water.
- Mix in a cup of soap flakes to a litre of warm water. Mix well and allow to stand until slightly thickened. Use whisks, sponges and spoons. The more it's whisked the more froth you will create. Children love playing with this 'slime' and its slippery texture. Colouring may be added if desired.
- Add a large lump of clay to a bowl of water. Allow the children to squash and squeeze the clay as it becomes more and more malleable. Very messy but very good fun!
- Add ice to a container of lukewarm water. A handful of ice-cubes is fun, but it is even better to add large lumps of ice. Freeze a plastic box of water, with or without colouring, and add the 'iceberg' to the water. Balloons filled with water and frozen produce great balloon-shaped ice blocks, which melt slowly. Great for outside on a hot day. Rubber gloves filled with water and frozen provide lots of fun shapes. Small objects (plastic animals are good) can be frozen into the blocks of ice and provide a talking point.
- Cornflour mixed with water (1 pack of cornflour to approx. 1 cup of water) makes a miraculous substance often referred to as 'gloop'. Scientifically speaking it produces a 'thixotropic' substance, not quite a liquid or a solid. Great fun to plunge your hands in and explore.

Vocabulary/discussion

- Children engaged in play of this kind provide an excellent opportunity for a practitioner to observe their reasoning, ability to negotiate, descriptive language skills and knowledge and understanding of the world. Careful intervention from an adult can maximise the development of these skills

Group size
Flexible

Extension ideas

1. Link water to its practical applications – flowers and plants, animals and birds.
2. What would happen to us if we had no water?

Links to Foundation Stage Curriculum

KUW Investigate objects and materials using all their senses as appropriate. Ask questions about why things happen and how things work. Observe, find out about and identify features in the place they live and in the natural world

CLL Use talk to organise, sequence and clarify thinking, ideas, feelings and events

CD Respond in a variety of ways to what they see, hear, smell, touch and feel

Health and safety

⚠ Take care that soap does not get into eyes. Flush thoroughly with cold water if splashes occur

⚠ Use only non-toxic food colouring

⚠ 'Gloop' and 'slime' do not keep, and will need to be disposed of at the end of a session

ACTIVITY

25 Natural collections

Resources you will need

- Large collections of shells, smooth pebbles, 'sea glass', smooth small pieces of pottery (glazed and unglazed), small pieces of driftwood, fir cones, conkers
- Torches and/or an overhead projector can be a fun addition

Aims/concepts

- Many of the activities undertaken in early years education rely upon resources for counting, sorting and so on. There are hundreds of such collections available commercially, most in primary coloured plastic. The same results can be achieved by providing the children with collections of natural materials. These have the advantage of being free, but do require time and patience to acquire. Get into the habit of beachcombing. One of the nicest resources is a collection of 'sea glass' (i.e. small chippings of glass that have been buffed by the sea and sand until they become smooth-edged and milky in appearance. These can be found in clear, green and brown, providing an excellent sorting resource). The beach is also a good hunting ground for small pieces of pottery made smooth and safe in the same way. Shells can be used for all sorting, counting and ordering activities as well as providing an excellent introduction to shape activities, where it is beneficial to look at the variety of shapes to be found in the natural environment rather than going straight to a collection of regular shapes
- The variety to be found in collections of this kind encourages the children to take time studying the materials. They note small differences between seemingly similar shells, pebbles and so on, and are more likely to choose their own criteria for sorting activities

Process

- Allow the children time to explore the collections in their own way. You may find that the children begin to sort or order naturally without adult intervention.
- Provide sorting grids or trays for the children to enable them to become more sophisticated in their work. The inside tray from a box of chocolates provides an excellent resource for children to fill with individual pieces from the collections. They could work collaboratively, each choosing a favourite piece to go into the box.
- Let the children use magnifying glasses or torches to examine the pieces closely. If available, an overhead projector may be used to see the objects displayed on a larger scale. This is particularly good for viewing the pieces of glass, as the light enhances the colours. If you are lucky enough to have a 'light table' this can really make the most of the collections.
- Use the collections for counting and ordering activities, for weighing and comparing, for shape and measure.
- Use for pattern-making. If an adult begins a repeating pattern can the children continue it?
- Add the glass, pottery or pebbles to water and notice how they change appearance.

Vocabulary/discussion

- The collections are so flexible in their use that the vocabulary and discussions developed will depend largely on the specific aim of the activity
- Specific mathematical language can be explored, creative activities undertaken and discussed
- Try asking the children what they think the pieces are, and where they think they come from

Group size

Flexible

Links to Foundation Stage Curriculum

CLL Interact with others, negotiating plans and activities and taking turns in conversation. Use talk to organise, sequence and clarify thinking, ideas, feelings and events

KUW Investigate objects and materials by using all their senses as appropriate. Look closely at similarities, differences, patterns and changes

CD Respond in a variety of ways to what they see, hear, smell, touch and feel. Express and communicate their ideas, thoughts and feelings by using a widening range of materials, imaginative and role-play, movement, designing and making

MD Use developing mathematical ideas and methods to solve practical problems:
- In practical activities and discussion begin to use the vocabulary involved in adding and subtracting
- Say and use number names in order in familiar contexts
- Count reliably up to ten everyday objects
- Find one more or one less than a number from one to ten
- Begin to relate addition to combining two groups of objects and subtraction to 'taking away'
- Use language such as 'greater', 'smaller', 'heavier' or 'lighter' to compare quantities
- Talk about, recognise and re-create simple patterns

PD Handle objects with increasing control. Use a range of small and large equipment with increasing control

Extension idea

The collections can be used purposefully for activities throughout Foundation Stage and KS1.

Health and safety

⚠ Check that pottery and glass are properly weathered and have no sharp edges

⚠ Wash the collected material well in water and detergent before allowing the children access to them

Photocopiable sheets

Sample risk assessment

Risk/hazard	Likelihood	Action
Eating poisonous plants	Low	Talk to children regarding health and safety rules prior to activity. Ensure that adults are aware of any toxic plants. Maintain adult supervision.
Access to main road	Medium	Talk to children regarding health and safety rules prior to activity. Keep gates and access point locked. Maintain adult supervision.
Cuts and abrasions	Medium	Pre-warn children of obvious hazards. Bring first aid kit.
Hay fever/asthma symptoms increase in open or wooded areas	Seasonal	Ensure that supervising adults are aware of any children with a condition. Bring appropriate medication.
Soil-borne bacterial infection	Low	Talk to children regarding health and safety rules prior to activity. Wash hands thoroughly after activity.

Risk assessment

Risk/hazard	Likelihood	Action

Woodland folk outline: Fairy

Woodland folk outline: Elf

Nature palettes

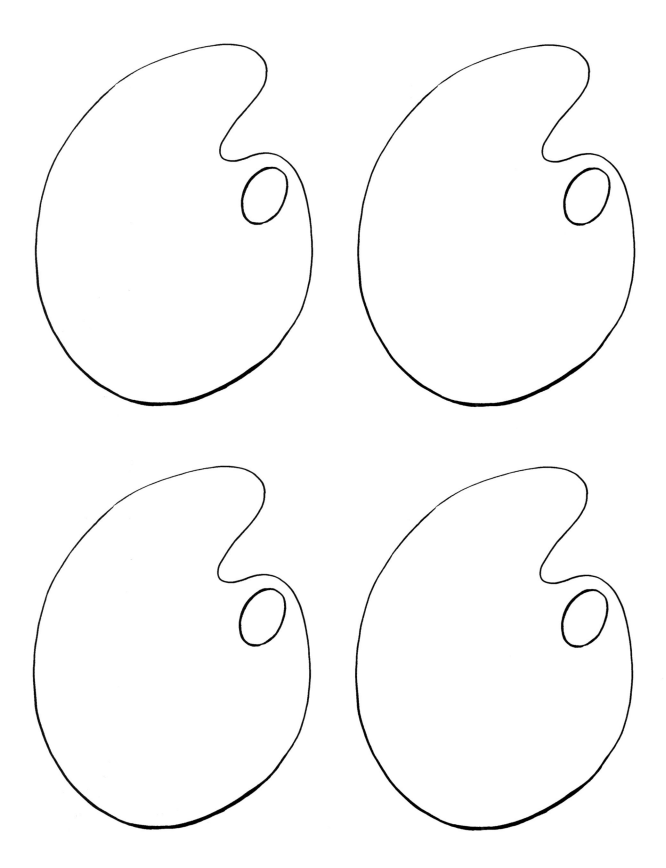

My bark rubbing

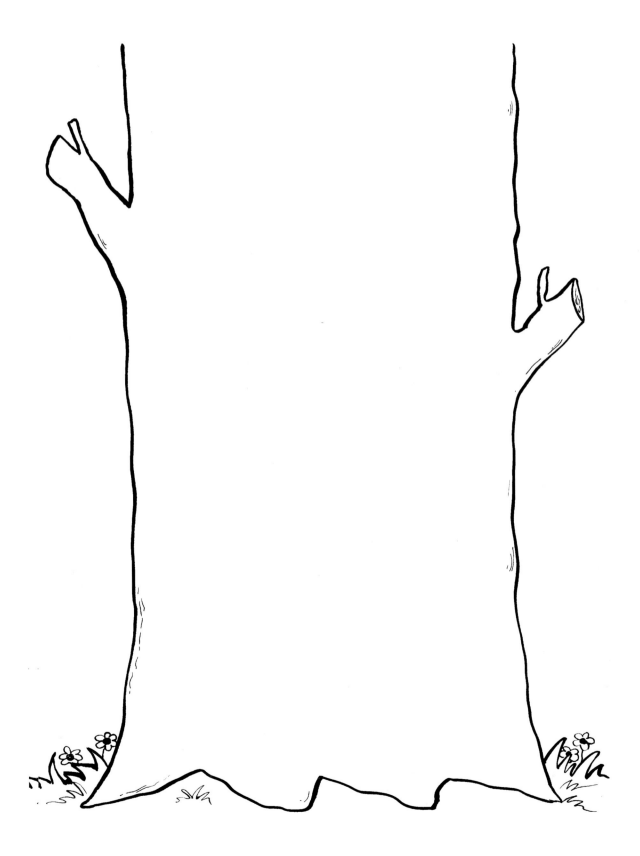

Growing seeds – discussion pictures

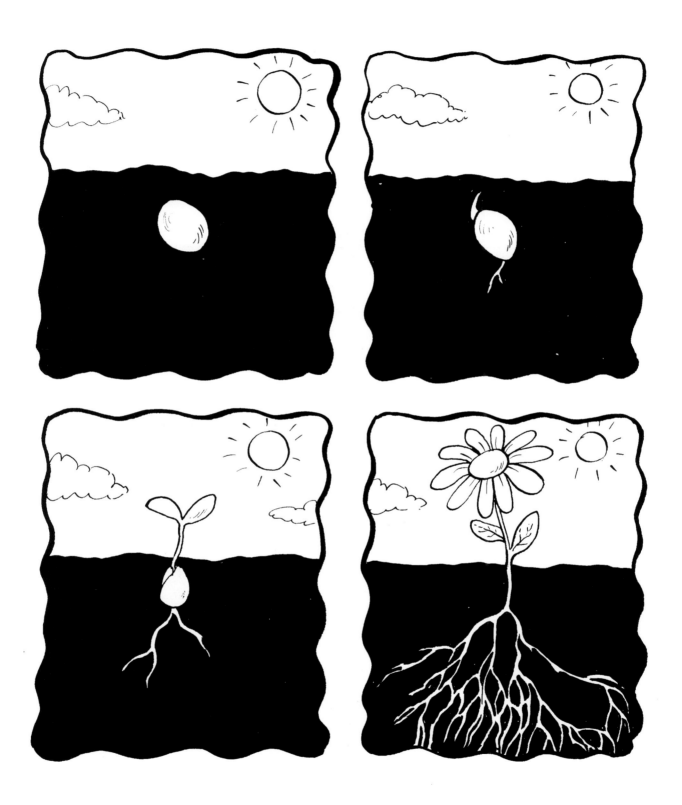

Paper spinner

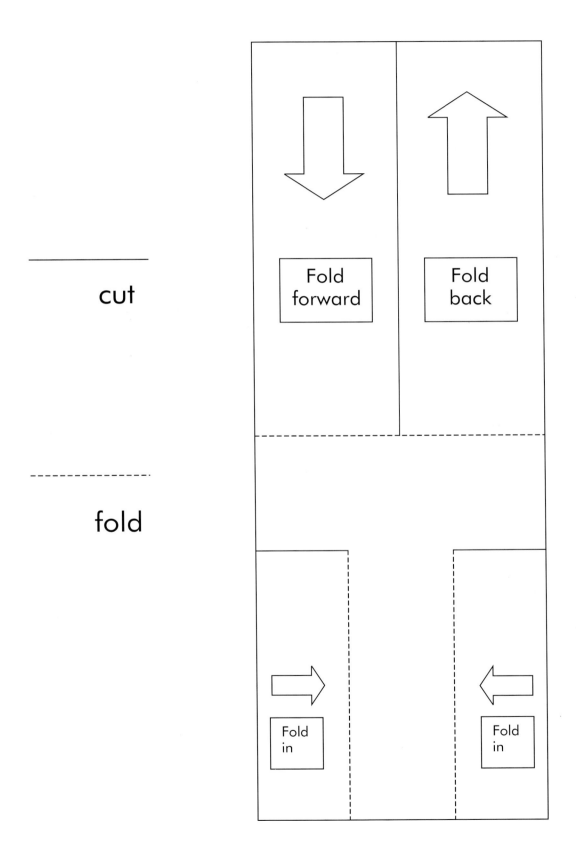

cut

fold

NB: Add a paper clip to the bottom of the spinner

Photocopiable sheet 9

Sorting rings

Label your circles according to activity, e.g.

living/not living
green/not green
rough/smooth
hard/soft
bigger/smaller
petal/leaf

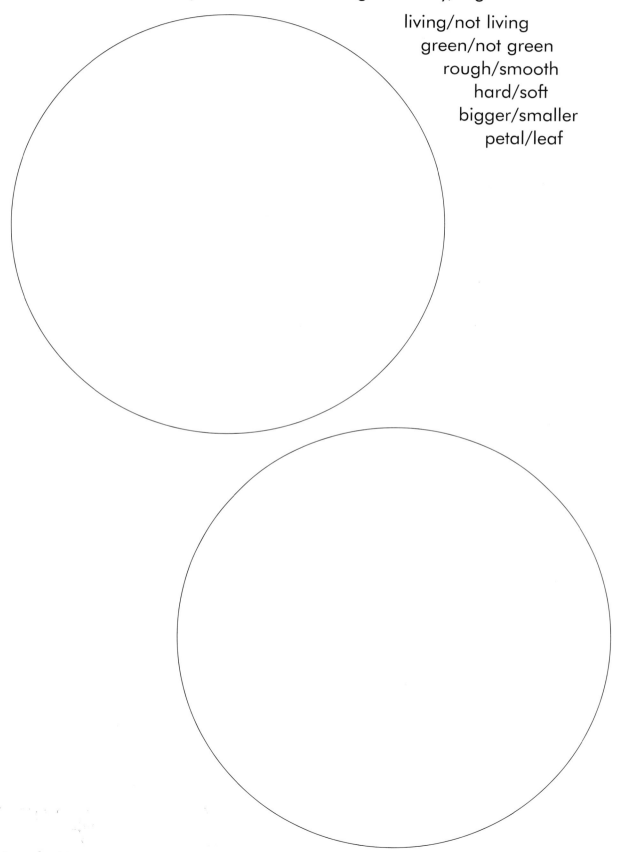

Resources

Useful resources, suppliers and websites

The Consortium (www.theconsortium.co.uk) sells shells by the bag, feathers, clay (including 'newclay'), magnifying glasses and sturdy two-way viewers.

NES Arnold (www.nesarnold.co.uk) sells shells, feathers, clay, viewers and gardening equipment. It also has a good selection of photopacks for use with children.

www.livingdesigns.co.uk is a company selling shells by the basket or bag. It also sells tumbled gemstones.

www.kereds.co.uk sells glass beads, feathers and withies.

www.catchingthelight.co.uk sells bags of 'sea glass'.

Withies are often available from small ads at the back of gardening magazines. The English Hurdle Curload (Stoke St Gregory, Taunton, Somerset TA3 6UD) sells withies through mail order.

Further reading

Non-fiction

Dan Davies and Alan Howe (2002), *Teaching Science and Design and Technology in the Early Years* (London: David Fulton)

Sam Godwin (2001), *From Little Acorns: A First Look at the Life Cycle of a Tree.* (London: Hodder)

Sam Godwin and Simon Abel (1998), *A Seed in Need: A First Look at the Life Cycle of a Flower* (London: Hodder)

Andy Goldsworthy: Books of photos, published by Viking:

- *Stone* (1994)
- *Wood* (1996)
- *Wall* (2000)

Lynn Higgins (2003): First Hand Science series, published by Franklin Watts:

- *Plants and Flowers*
- *Water*
- *Materials*
- *Seashore*
- *Weather*

Henry Pluckrose (1998): Senses series, published by Franklin Watts:

- *Looking and Seeing*
- *Listening and Hearing*
- *Eating and Tasting*

The Spotty Zebra guided reading scheme covers various non-fiction books and activities linked with fiction books (Cheltenham: Nelson Thornes).

Fiction

Eileen Browne (1995), *Handa's Surprise* (London: Walker Books)

Malachy Doyle (1999), *Jody's Beans* (London: Walker Books)

Vivian French and Alison Bartlett (1995), *Oliver's Vegetables* (London: Walker Books)

Sally Grindley and Susan Varley (2003), *Why is the Sky Blue?* (London: Andersen Press)

Shirley Hughes (2001), *Alfie's Weather* (London: The Bodley Head)

Simon James (2003), *The Wild Woods* (London: Walker Books)

Websites

www.naturegrid.org

CD-ROMs

2Simple Science Simulation Module 1: Plants and Growing. 2Simple, 3–4 Sentinel Square, Brent Street, London NW4 2EL (www.2simple.com)

Garden Wildlife. Anglia Multimedia (www.anglia.co.uk)

The Seasons of Little Brown Bear. Sherston Software. Sherston Publishing Group, Angel House, Sherston, Nr Malmsbury, Wiltshire SN16 0LH